HAL•LEONARD

JAZZ PLAY-ALONG

Book and CD for B♭, E♭, C and Bass Clef Instruments

volume 140

Arranged and Produced by Mark Taylor and Jim Roberts

BOOK

TITLE	PAGE NUMBERS			
	C Treble Instruments	B♭ Instruments	E♭ Instruments	C Bass Instruments
Baby That's What I Need (Walk Tall)	7	23	39	55
Birdland	4	20	36	52
Black Market	8	24	40	56
In a Silent Way	9	25	41	57
Man in the Green Shirt	10	26	42	58
Mercy, Mercy, Mercy	12	28	44	60
Midnight Mood	14	30	46	62
Money in the Pocket	13	29	45	61
One Man's Dream	16	32	48	64
Scotch and Water	18	34	50	66

CD

TITLE	CD Track Number Split Track/Melody	CD Track Number Full Stereo Track
Baby That's What I Need (Walk Tall)	19	20
Birdland	1	2
Black Market	3	4
In a Silent Way	5	6
Man in the Green Shirt	7	8
Mercy, Mercy, Mercy	9	10
Midnight Mood	11	12
Money in the Pocket	13	14
One Man's Dream	15	16
Scotch and Water	17	18
B♭ Tuning Notes		21

COVER PHOTO ©AVEPILDAS/CTSIMAGES

ISBN 978-1-4234-9455-3

HAL•LEONARD®
CORPORATION

7777 W. BLUEMOUND RD. P.O. BOX 13819 MILWAUKEE, WI 53213

D0504056

Visit Hal Leonard Online at
www.halleonard.com

JOE ZAWINUL

Volume 140

Arranged and Produced by
Mark Taylor and Jim Roberts

Featured Players:

Graham Breedlove–Trumpet
John Desalme–Sax
Tony Nalker–Piano
Jim Roberts–Bass
Todd Harrison–Drums

Recorded at Bias Studios, Springfield, Virginia
Bob Dawson, Engineer

HOW TO USE THE CD:

Each song has <u>two</u> tracks:

1) Split Track/Melody

Woodwind, Brass, Keyboard, and **Mallet Players** can use this track as a learning tool for melody style and inflection.

Bass Players can learn and perform with this track – remove the recorded bass track by turning down the volume on the LEFT channel.

Keyboard and **Guitar Players** can learn and perform with this track – remove the recorded piano part by turning down the volume on the RIGHT channel.

2) Full Stereo Track

Soloists or **Groups** can learn and perform with this accompaniment track with the RHYTHM SECTION only.

BIRDLAND

BY JOSEF ZAWINUL

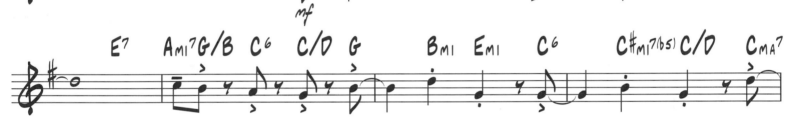

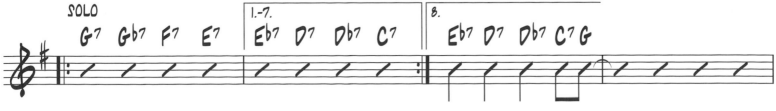

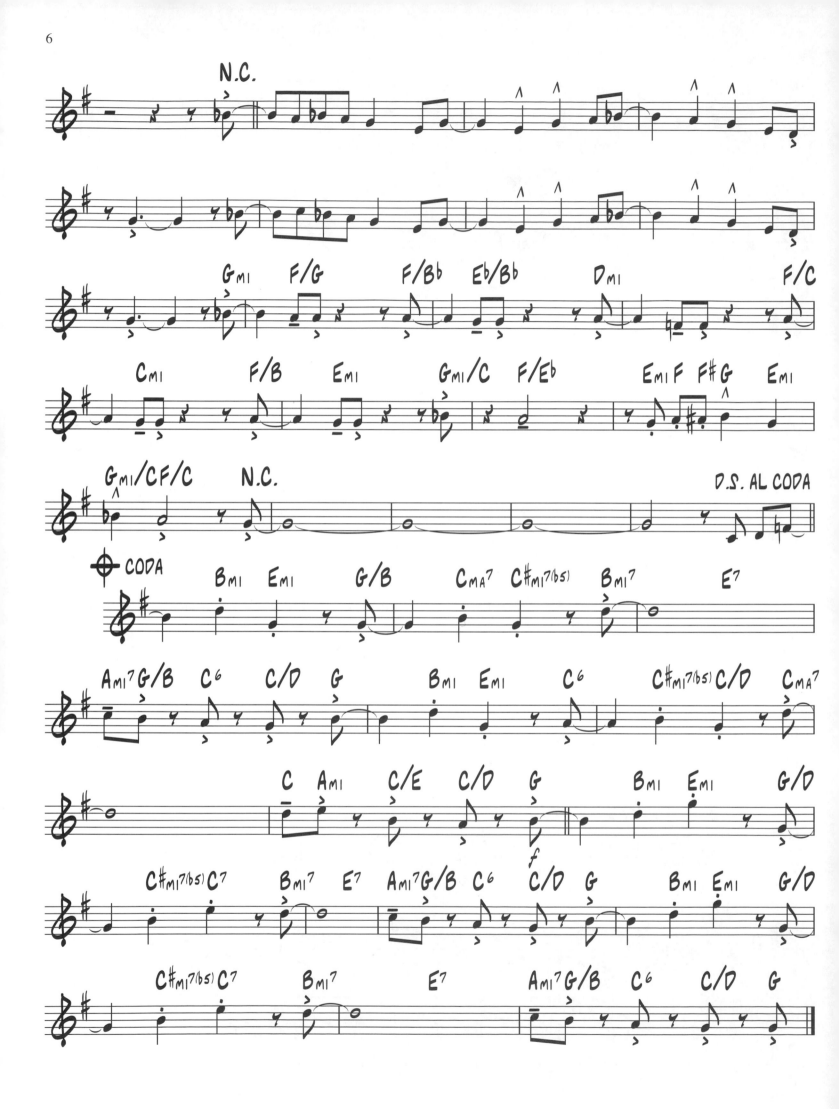

BABY THAT'S WHAT I NEED
(WALK TALL)

BY JOSEF ZAWINUL, ESTHER MARROW AND JAMES REIN

CD

19: SPLIT TRACK/MELODY
20: FULL STEREO TRACK

C VERSION

BLACK MARKET

BY JOSEF ZAWINUL

C VERSION

IN A SILENT WAY

BY JOSEF ZAWINUL

CD
5 : SPLIT TRACK/MELODY
6 : FULL STEREO TRACK

C VERSION

MAN IN THE GREEN SHIRT

BY JOSEF ZAWINUL

MERCY, MERCY, MERCY

CD
◆ 9 : SPLIT TRACK/MELODY
◆ 10 : FULL STEREO TRACK

BY JOSEF ZAWINUL

C VERSION

MONEY IN THE POCKET

C VERSION

BY JOSEF ZAWINUL

MIDNIGHT MOOD

BY JOSEF ZAWINUL

CD

- **11** : SPLIT TRACK/MELODY
- **12** : FULL STEREO TRACK

C VERSION

MEDIUM JAZZ WALTZ

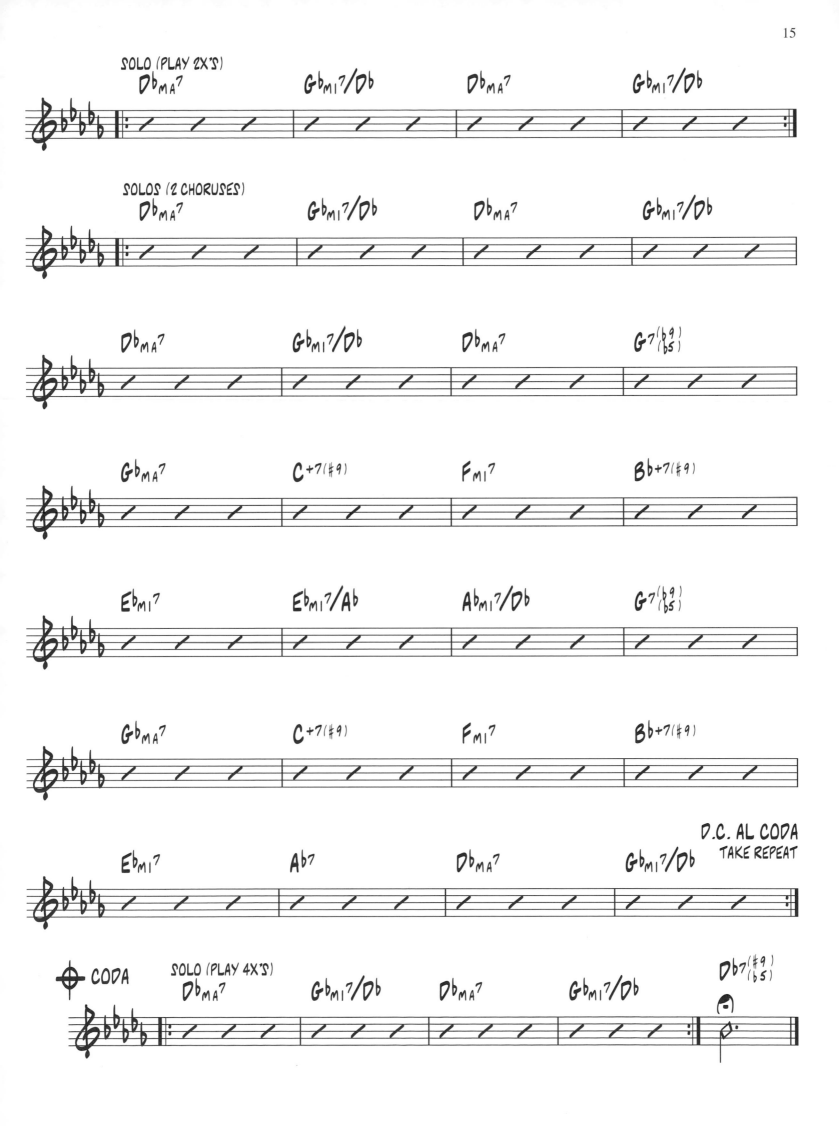

CD

🔶15 : SPLIT TRACK/MELODY
🔶16 : FULL STEREO TRACK

ONE MAN'S DREAM

BY JOSEF ZAWINUL
AND CHARLES WRIGHT

C VERSION

SCOTCH AND WATER

BY JOE ZAWINUL

C VERSION

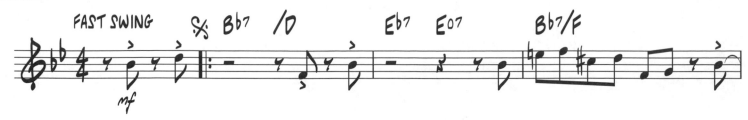

SOLOS (2 CHORUSES)

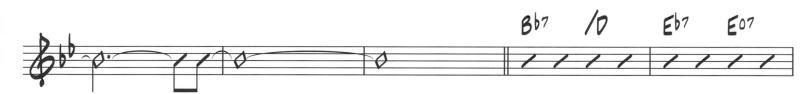

D.S. AL CODA
TAKE REPEAT

LAST X ONLY

BIRDLAND

BY JOSEF ZAWINUL

①: SPLIT TRACK/MELODY
②: FULL STEREO TRACK

Bb VERSION

E PEDAL — F# PEDAL — — D PEDAL — —

TO CODA ⊕

A7

Bb7

A7

f

Bb7   A7   C#mi7(b5)

A   C#mi F#mi   A/C#   DMA7 D#mi7(b5) C#mi7

mf

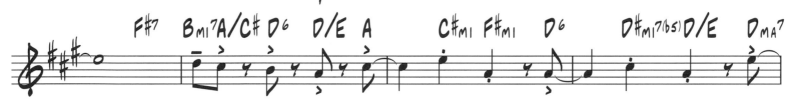

F#7 Bmi7A/C# D6 D/E A   C#mi F#mi   D6   D#mi7(b5)D/E   DMA7

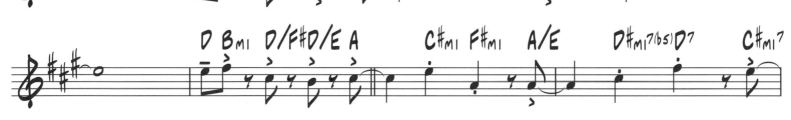

D Bmi D/F#D/E A   C#mi F#mi   A/E   D#mi7(b5)D7   C#mi7

F#7 Bmi7A/C# D6 D/E A   C#mi F#mi   A/E   D#mi7(b5)D7   C#mi7

F#7 Bmi7A/C#D6 D/E A

N.C.

1ST X ONLY

SOLO
A7 Ab7 G7 F#7

1.-7.
F7 E7 Eb7 D7

8.
F7 E7 Eb7 D7 A

BABY THAT'S WHAT I NEED
(WALK TALL)

BY JOSEF ZAWINUL,
ESTHER MARROW AND JAMES REIN

BLACK MARKET

BY JOSEF ZAWINUL

IN A SILENT WAY

BY JOSEF ZAWINUL

CD
◆5: SPLIT TRACK/MELODY
◆6: FULL STEREO TRACK

Bb VERSION

MAN IN THE GREEN SHIRT

BY JOSEF ZAWINUL

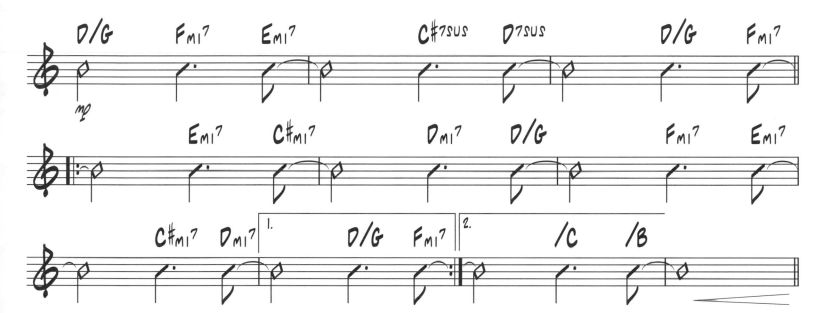

MERCY, MERCY, MERCY

BY JOSEF ZAWINUL

Bb VERSION

MONEY IN THE POCKET

BY JOSEF ZAWINUL

MIDNIGHT MOOD

BY JOSEF ZAWINUL

Bb VERSION

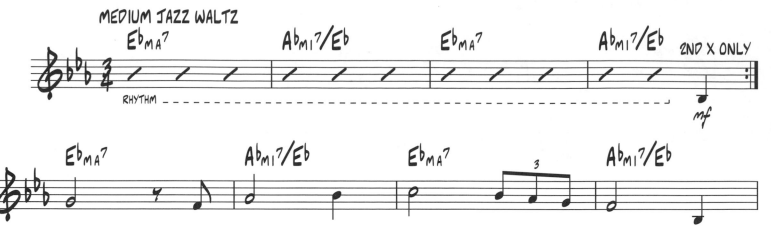

SOLO (PLAY 2X'S)

SOLOS (2 CHORUSES)

D.C. AL CODA
TAKE REPEAT

CODA

SOLO (PLAY 4X'S)

ONE MAN'S DREAM

BY JOSEF ZAWINUL
AND CHARLES WRIGHT

SCOTCH AND WATER

BY JOE ZAWINUL

CD
17: SPLIT TRACK/MELODY
18: FULL STEREO TRACK

Bb VERSION

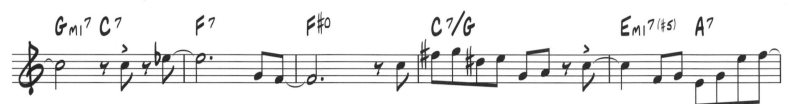

SOLOS (2 CHORUSES)

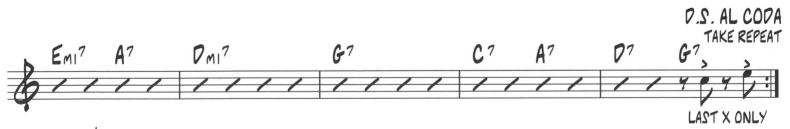

BIRDLAND

BY JOSEF ZAWINUL

CD
19: SPLIT TRACK/MELODY
20: FULL STEREO TRACK

BABY THAT'S WHAT I NEED
(WALK TALL)

BY JOSEF ZAWINUL,
ESTHER MARROW AND JAMES REIN

Eb VERSION

BLACK MARKET

BY JOSEF ZAWINUL

CD
3 : SPLIT TRACK/MELODY
4 : FULL STEREO TRACK

Eb VERSION

IN A SILENT WAY

By Josef Zawinul

CD
◆7: SPLIT TRACK/MELODY
◆8: FULL STEREO TRACK

MAN IN THE GREEN SHIRT

BY JOSEF ZAWINUL

Eb VERSION

MERCY, MERCY, MERCY

BY JOSEF ZAWINUL

MONEY IN THE POCKET

BY JOSEF ZAWINUL

CD
13: SPLIT TRACK/MELODY
14: FULL STEREO TRACK

Eb VERSION

MIDNIGHT MOOD

By Josef Zawinul

Eb VERSION

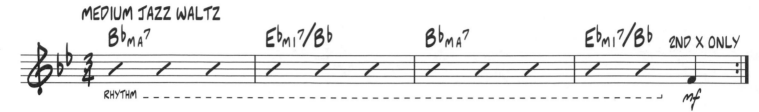

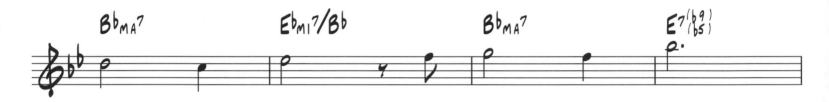

SOLO (PLAY 2X'S)
Bb MA7 | Ebmi7/Bb | BbMA7 | Ebmi7/Bb

SOLOS (2 CHORUSES)
BbMA7 | Ebmi7/Bb | BbMA7 | Ebmi7/Bb

BbMA7 | Ebmi7/Bb | BbMA7 | E7(b9)(b5)

EbMA7 | A+7(#9) | Dmi7 | G+7(#9)

Cmi7 | Cmi7/F | Fmi7/Bb | E7(b9)(b5)

EbMA7 | A+7(#9) | Dmi7 | G+7(#9)

D.C. AL CODA
TAKE REPEAT

Cmi7 | F7 | BbMA7 | Ebmi7/Bb

CODA
SOLO (PLAY 4X'S)
BbMA7 | Ebmi7/Bb | BbMA7 | Ebmi7/Bb | Bb7(#9)(b5)

ONE MAN'S DREAM

BY JOSEF ZAWINUL
AND CHARLES WRIGHT

CD
17 : SPLIT TRACK/MELODY
18 : FULL STEREO TRACK

SCOTCH AND WATER

BY JOE ZAWINUL

Eb VERSION

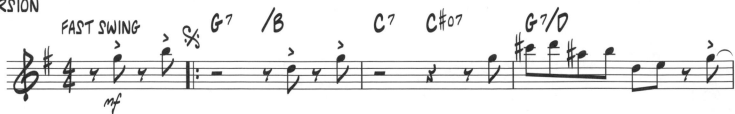

SOLOS (2 CHORUSES)

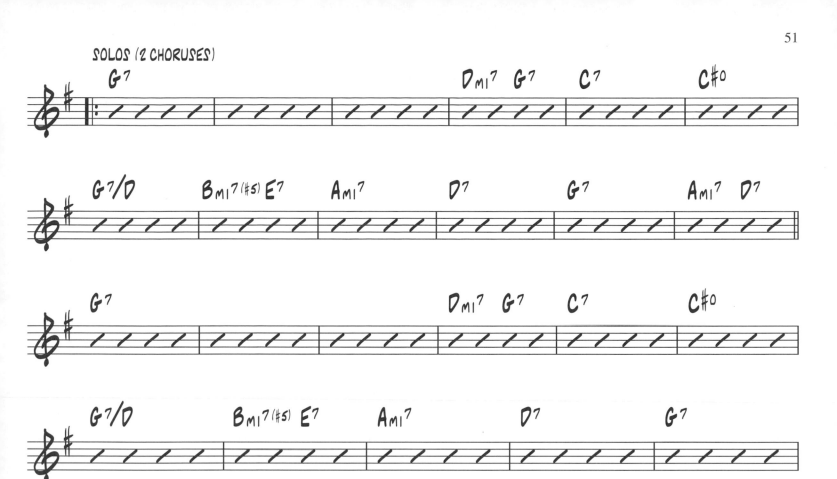

D.S. AL CODA
TAKE REPEAT

LAST X ONLY

BIRDLAND

1 : SPLIT TRACK/MELODY
2 : FULL STEREO TRACK

BY JOSEF ZAWINUL

C VERSION

BLACK MARKET

BY JOSEF ZAWINUL

𝄢: C VERSION

IN A SILENT WAY

BY JOSEF ZAWINUL

MAN IN THE GREEN SHIRT

BY JOSEF ZAWINUL

MERCY, MERCY, MERCY

BY JOSEF ZAWINUL

MONEY IN THE POCKET

BY JOSEF ZAWINUL

CD
13 : SPLIT TRACK/MELODY
14 : FULL STEREO TRACK

C VERSION
MEDIUM SOUL JAZZ

MIDNIGHT MOOD

BY JOSEF ZAWINUL

𝄢: C VERSION

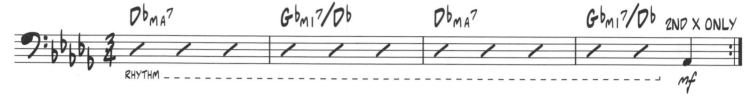

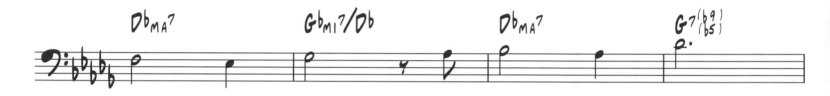

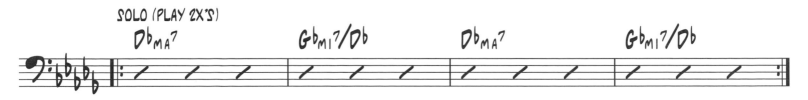

SOLO (PLAY 2X'S)
| Dbma7 | Gbmi7/Db | Dbma7 | Gbmi7/Db |

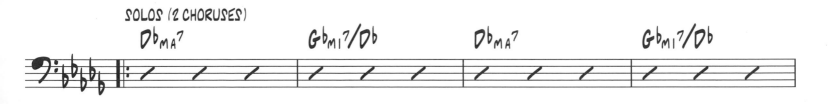

SOLOS (2 CHORUSES)
| Dbma7 | Gbmi7/Db | Dbma7 | Gbmi7/Db |

| Dbma7 | Gbmi7/Db | Dbma7 | G7(b9)(b5) |

| Gbma7 | C+7(#9) | Fmi7 | Bb+7(#9) |

| Ebmi7 | Ebmi7/Ab | Abmi7/Db | G7(b9)(b5) |

| Gbma7 | C+7(#9) | Fmi7 | Bb+7(#9) |

D.C. AL CODA
TAKE REPEAT
| Ebmi7 | Ab7 | Dbma7 | Gbmi7/Db |

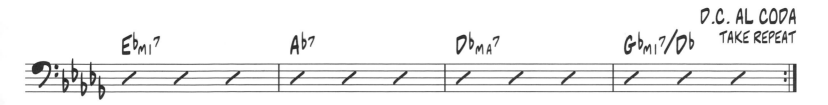

CODA
SOLO (PLAY 4X'S)
| Dbma7 | Gbmi7/Db | Dbma7 | Gbmi7/Db | Db7(#9)(b5) |

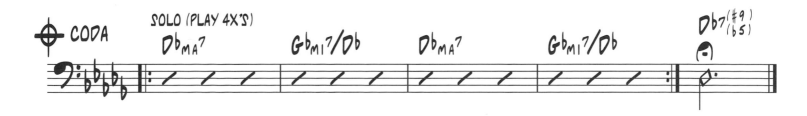

ONE MAN'S DREAM

BY JOSEF ZAWINUL
AND CHARLES WRIGHT

SCOTCH AND WATER

BY JOE ZAWINUL

CD
17 : SPLIT TRACK/MELODY
18 : FULL STEREO TRACK

𝄢: C VERSION

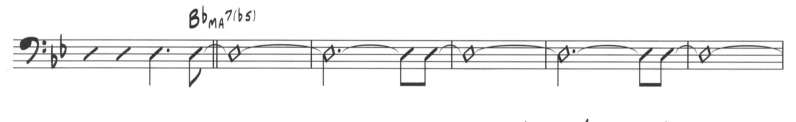

Presenting the Hal Leonard JAZZ PLAY-ALONG SERIES

For use with all B-flat, E-flat, Bass Clef and C instruments, the Jazz Play-Along® Series is the ultimate learning tool for all jazz musicians. With musician-friendly lead sheets, melody cues, and other split-track choices on the included CD, these first-of-a-kind packages help you master improvisation while playing some of the greatest tunes of all time. FOR STUDY, each tune includes a split track with: melody cue with proper style and inflection • professional rhythm tracks • choruses for soloing • removable bass part • removable piano part. FOR PERFORMANCE, each tune also has: an additional full stereo accompaniment track (no melody) • additional choruses for soloing.

1. **DUKE ELLINGTON**
00841644.........................$16.95

1A. **MAIDEN VOYAGE/ALL BLUES**
00843158 ....$15.99

2. **MILES DAVIS**
00841645.........................$16.95

3. **THE BLUES**
00841646.........................$16.99

4. **JAZZ BALLADS**
00841691.........................$16.99

5. **BEST OF BEBOP**
00841689.........................$16.95

6. **JAZZ CLASSICS WITH EASY CHANGES**
00841690.........................$16.99

7. **ESSENTIAL JAZZ STANDARDS**
00843000.........................$16.99

8. **ANTONIO CARLOS JOBIM AND THE ART OF THE BOSSA NOVA**
00843001 ....$16.95

9. **DIZZY GILLESPIE**
00843002.........................$16.99

10. **DISNEY CLASSICS**
00843003.........................$16.99

11. **RODGERS AND HART FAVORITES**
00843004.........................$16.99

12. **ESSENTIAL JAZZ CLASSICS**
00843005.........................$16.99

13. **JOHN COLTRANE**
00843006.........................$16.95

14. **IRVING BERLIN**
00843007.........................$15.99

15. **RODGERS & HAMMERSTEIN**
00843008.........................$15.99

16. **COLE PORTER**
00843009.........................$15.95

17. **COUNT BASIE**
00843010.........................$16.95

18. **HAROLD ARLEN**
00843011.........................$15.95

19. **COOL JAZZ**
00843012.........................$15.95

20. **CHRISTMAS CAROLS**
00843080.........................$14.95

21. **RODGERS AND HART CLASSICS**
00843014.........................$14.95

22. **WAYNE SHORTER**
00843015.........................$16.95

23. **LATIN JAZZ**
00843016.........................$16.95

24. **EARLY JAZZ STANDARDS**
00843017.........................$14.95

25. **CHRISTMAS JAZZ**
00843018.........................$16.95

26. **CHARLIE PARKER**
00843019.........................$16.95

27. **GREAT JAZZ STANDARDS**
00843020.........................$16.99

28. **BIG BAND ERA**
00843021.........................$15.99

29. **LENNON AND MCCARTNEY**
00843022.........................$16.95

30. **BLUES' BEST**
00843023.........................$15.99

31. **JAZZ IN THREE**
00843024.........................$15.99

32. **BEST OF SWING**
00843025.........................$15.99

33. **SONNY ROLLINS**
00843029.........................$15.95

34. **ALL TIME STANDARDS**
00843030.........................$15.99

35. **BLUESY JAZZ**
00843031.........................$16.99

36. **HORACE SILVER**
00843032.........................$16.99

37. **BILL EVANS**
00843033.........................$16.95

38. **YULETIDE JAZZ**
00843034.........................$16.95

39. **"ALL THE THINGS YOU ARE" & MORE JEROME KERN SONGS**
00843035.........................$15.99

40. **BOSSA NOVA**
00843036.........................$15.99

41. **CLASSIC DUKE ELLINGTON**
00843037.........................$16.99

42. **GERRY MULLIGAN FAVORITES**
00843038.........................$16.99

43. **GERRY MULLIGAN CLASSICS**
00843039.........................$16.95

44. **OLIVER NELSON**
00843040.........................$16.95

45. **JAZZ AT THE MOVIES**
00843041.........................$15.99

46. **BROADWAY JAZZ STANDARDS**
00843042.........................$15.99

47. **CLASSIC JAZZ BALLADS**
00843043.........................$15.99

48. **BEBOP CLASSICS**
00843044.........................$16.99

49. **MILES DAVIS STANDARDS**
00843045.........................$16.95

50. **GREAT JAZZ CLASSICS**
00843046.........................$15.99

51. **UP-TEMPO JAZZ**
00843047.........................$15.99

52. **STEVIE WONDER**
00843048.........................$16.99

53. **RHYTHM CHANGES**
00843049.........................$15.99

54. **"MOONLIGHT IN VERMONT" AND OTHER GREAT STANDARDS**
00843050.........................$15.99

55. **BENNY GOLSON**
00843052.........................$15.95

56. **"GEORGIA ON MY MIND" & OTHER SONGS BY HOAGY CARMICHAEL**
00843056 ....$15.99

57. **VINCE GUARALDI**
00843057.........................$16.99

58. **MORE LENNON AND MCCARTNEY**
00843059.........................$15.99

59. **SOUL JAZZ**
00843060.........................$15.99

60. **DEXTER GORDON**
00843061 ....$15.95

61. **MONGO SANTAMARIA**
00843062.........................$15.95

62. **JAZZ-ROCK FUSION**
00843063.........................$16.99

63. CLASSICAL JAZZ
00843064 ....$14.95

64. TV TUNES
00843065 ....$14.95

65. SMOOTH JAZZ
00843066 ....$16.99

66. A CHARLIE BROWN CHRISTMAS
00843067 ....$16.99

67. CHICK COREA
00843068 ....$15.95

68. CHARLES MINGUS
00843069 ....$16.95

69. CLASSIC JAZZ
00843071 ....$15.99

70. THE DOORS
00843072 ....$14.95

71. COLE PORTER CLASSICS
00843073 ....$14.95

72. CLASSIC JAZZ BALLADS
00843074 ....$15.99

73. JAZZ/BLUES
00843075 ....$14.95

74. BEST JAZZ CLASSICS
00843076 ....$15.99

75. PAUL DESMOND
00843077 ....$14.95

76. BROADWAY JAZZ BALLADS
00843078 ....$15.99

77. JAZZ ON BROADWAY
00843079 ....$15.99

78. STEELY DAN
00843070 ....$14.99

79. MILES DAVIS CLASSICS
00843081 ....$15.99

80. JIMI HENDRIX
00843083 ....$15.99

81. FRANK SINATRA – CLASSICS
00843084 ....$15.99

82. FRANK SINATRA – STANDARDS
00843085 ....$15.99

83. ANDREW LLOYD WEBBER
00843104 ....$14.95

84. BOSSA NOVA CLASSICS
00843105 ....$14.95

85. MOTOWN HITS
00843109 ....$14.95

86. BENNY GOODMAN
00843110 ....$14.95

87. DIXIELAND
00843111 ....$14.95

88. DUKE ELLINGTON FAVORITES
00843112 ....$14.95

89. IRVING BERLIN FAVORITES
00843113 ....$14.95

90. THELONIOUS MONK CLASSICS
00841262 ....$16.99

91. THELONIOUS MONK FAVORITES
00841263 ....$16.99

92. LEONARD BERNSTEIN
00450134 ....$15.99

93. DISNEY FAVORITES
00843142 ....$14.99

94. RAY
00843143 ....$14.99

95. JAZZ AT THE LOUNGE
00843144 ....V$14.99

96. LATIN JAZZ STANDARDS
00843145 ....$14.99

97. MAYBE I'M AMAZED★
00843148 ....$15.99

98. DAVE FRISHBERG
00843149 ....$15.99

99. SWINGING STANDARDS
00843150 ....$14.99

100. LOUIS ARMSTRONG
00740423 ....$15.99

101. BUD POWELL
00843152 ....$14.99

102. JAZZ POP
00843153 ....$14.99

**103. ON GREEN DOLPHIN STREET
& OTHER JAZZ CLASSICS**
00843154 ....$14.99

104. ELTON JOHN
00843155 ....$14.99

105. SOULFUL JAZZ
00843151 ....$15.99

106. SLO' JAZZ
00843117 ....$14.99

107. MOTOWN CLASSICS
00843116 ....$14.99

108. JAZZ WALTZ
00843159 ....$15.99

109. OSCAR PETERSON
00843160 ....$16.99

110. JUST STANDARDS
00843161 ....$15.99

111. COOL CHRISTMAS
00843162 ....$15.99

112. PAQUITO D'RIVERA – LATIN JAZZ★
48020662 ....$16.99

113. PAQUITO D'RIVERA – BRAZILIAN JAZZ★
48020663 ....$19.99

114. MODERN JAZZ QUARTET FAVORITES
00843163 ....$15.99

115. THE SOUND OF MUSIC
00843164 ....$15.99

116. JACO PASTORIUS
00843165 ....$15.99

117. ANTONIO CARLOS JOBIM – MORE HITS
00843166 ....$15.99

118. BIG JAZZ STANDARDS COLLECTION
00843167 ....$27.50

119. JELLY ROLL MORTON
00843168 ....$15.99

120. J.S. BACH
00843169 ....$15.99

121. DJANGO REINHARDT
00843170 ....$15.99

122. PAUL SIMON
00843182 ....$16.99

123. BACHARACH & DAVID
00843185 ....$15.99

124. JAZZ-ROCK HORN HITS
00843186 ....$15.99

126. COUNT BASIE CLASSICS
00843157 ....$15.99

127. CHUCK MANGIONE
00843188 ....$15.99

132. STAN GETZ ESSENTIALS
00843193 ....$15.99

133. STAN GETZ FAVORITES
00843194 ....$15.99

134. NURSERY RHYMES★
00843196 ....$17.99

135. JEFF BECK
00843197 ....$15.99

136. NAT ADDERLEY
00843198 ....$15.99

137. WES MONTGOMERY
00843199 ....$15.99

138. FREDDIE HUBBARD
00843200 ....$15.99

139. JULIAN "CANNONBALL" ADDERLEY
00843201 ....$15.99

141. BILL EVANS STANDARDS
00843156 ....$15.99

150. JAZZ IMPROV BASICS
00843195 ....$19.99

151. MODERN JAZZ QUARTET CLASSICS
00843209 ....$15.99

157. HYMNS
00843217 ....$15.99

162. BIG CHRISTMAS COLLECTION
00843221 ....$24.99

★These CDs do not include split tracks.

0811

Jazz Instruction & Improvisation
Books for All Instruments from Hal Leonard

AN APPROACH TO JAZZ IMPROVISATION
by Dave Pozzi
Musicians Institute Press
Explore the styles of Charlie Parker, Sonny Rollins, Bud Powell and others with this comprehensive guide to jazz improvisation. Covers: scale choices • chord analysis • phrasing • melodies • harmonic progressions • more.
00695135 Book/CD Pack $17.95

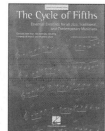

BUILDING A JAZZ VOCABULARY
By Mike Steinel
A valuable resource for learning the basics of jazz from Mike Steinel of the University of North Texas. It covers: the basics of jazz • how to build effective solos • a comprehensive practice routine • and a jazz vocabulary of the masters.
00849911 ....$19.95

THE CYCLE OF FIFTHS
by Emile and Laura De Cosmo
This essential instruction book provides more than 450 exercises, including hundreds of melodic and rhythmic ideas. The book is designed to help improvisors master the cycle of fifths, one of the primary progressions in music. Guaranteed to refine technique, enhance improvisational fluency, and improve sight-reading!
00311114 ....$16.99

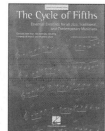

THE DIATONIC CYCLE
by Emile and Laura De Cosmo
Renowned jazz educators Emile and Laura De Cosmo provide more than 300 exercises to help improvisors tackle one of music's most common progressions: the diatonic cycle. This book is guaranteed to refine technique, enhance improvisational fluency, and improve sight-reading!
00311115 ....$16.95

EAR TRAINING
by Keith Wyatt, Carl Schroeder and Joe Elliott
Musicians Institute Press
Covers: basic pitch matching • singing major and minor scales • identifying intervals • transcribing melodies and rhythm • identifying chords and progressions • seventh chords and the blues • modal interchange, chromaticism, modulation • and more.
00695198 Book/2-CD Pack.......................$24.95

EXERCISES AND ETUDES FOR THE JAZZ INSTRUMENTALIST
by J.J. Johnson
Designed as study material and playable by any instrument, these pieces run the gamut of the jazz experience, featuring common and uncommon time signatures and keys, and styles from ballads to funk. They are progressively graded so that both beginners and professionals will be challenged by the demands of this wonderful music.
00842018 Bass Clef Edition...................$16.95
00842042 Treble Clef Edition $16.95

JAZZOLOGY
THE ENCYCLOPEDIA OF JAZZ THEORY FOR ALL MUSICIANS
by Robert Rawlins and Nor Eddine Bahha
This comprehensive resource covers a variety of jazz topics, for beginners and pros of any instrument. The book serves as an encyclopedia for reference, a thorough methodology for the student, and a workbook for the classroom.
00311167 ....$18.95

JAZZ JAM SESSION
15 TRACKS INCLUDING RHYTHM CHANGES, BLUES, BOSSA, BALLADS & MORE
by Ed Friedland
Bring your local jazz jam session home! These essential jazz rhythm grooves feature a professional rhythm section and are perfect for guitar, harmonica, keyboard, saxophone and trumpet players to hone their soloing skills. The feels, tempos and keys have been varied to broaden your jazz experience. Styles include: ballads, bebop, blues, bossa nova, cool jazz, and more, with improv guidelines for each track.
_____00311827 Book/CD Pack........................$19.99

JAZZ THEORY RESOURCES
by Bert Ligon
Houston Publishing, Inc.
This is a jazz theory text in two volumes. **Volume 1 includes:** review of basic theory • rhythm in jazz performance • triadic generalization • diatonic harmonic progressions and analysis • substitutions and turnarounds • and more. **Volume 2 includes:** modes and modal frameworks • quartal harmony • extended tertian structures and triadic superimposition • pentatonic applications • coloring "outside" the lines and beyond • and more.
00030458 Volume 1 ....$39.95
00030459 Volume 2 ....$29.95

JOY OF IMPROV
by Dave Frank and John Amaral
This book/CD course on improvisation for all instruments and all styles will help players develop monster musical skills! **Book One** imparts a solid basis in technique, rhythm, chord theory, ear training and improv concepts. **Book Two** explores more advanced chord voicings, chord arranging techniques and more challenging blues and melodic lines. The CD can be used as a listening and play-along tool.
00220005 Book 1 – Book/CD Pack $27.99
00220006 Book 2 – Book/CD Pack $24.95

THE PATH TO JAZZ IMPROVISATION
by Emile and Laura De Cosmo
This fascinating jazz instruction book offers an innovative, scholarly approach to the art of improvisation. It includes in-depth analysis and lessons about: cycle of fifths • diatonic cycle • overtone series • pentatonic scale • harmonic and melodic minor scale • polytonal order of keys • blues and bebop scales • modes • and more.
00310904 ....$14.95

THE SOURCE
THE DICTIONARY OF CONTEMPORARY AND TRADITIONAL SCALES
by Steve Barta
This book serves as an informative guide for people who are looking for good, solid information regarding scales, chords, and how they work together. It provides right and left hand fingerings for scales, chords, and complete inversions. Includes over 20 different scales, each written in all 12 keys.
00240885 ....$15.95

21 BEBOP EXERCISES
by Steve Rawlins
This book/CD pack is both a warm-up collection and a manual for bebop phrasing. Its tasty and sophisticated exercises will help you develop your proficiency with jazz interpretation. It concentrates on practice in all twelve keys – moving higher by half-step – to help develop dexterity and range. The companion CD includes all of the exercises in 12 keys.
00315341 Book/CD Pack $17.95

FOR MORE INFORMATION, SEE YOUR LOCAL MUSIC DEALER, OR WRITE TO:

HAL•LEONARD® CORPORATION
7777 W. BLUEMOUND RD. P.O. BOX 13819 MILWAUKEE, WI 53213

Prices, contents & availability subject to change without notice.

Visit Hal Leonard online at
www.halleonard.com

0910

ARTIST TRANSCRIPTIONS®

Artist Transcriptions are authentic, note-for-note transcriptions of today's hottest artists in jazz, pop and rock. These outstanding, accurate arrangements are in an easy-to-read format which includes all essential lines. Artist Transcriptions can be used to perform, sequence or for reference.

CLARINET

00672423	Buddy De Franco Collection	$19.95

FLUTE

00672379	Eric Dolphy Collection	$19.95
00672372	James Moody Collection – Sax and Flute	$19.95
00660108	James Newton – Improvising Flute	$14.95

GUITAR & BASS

00660113	The Guitar Style of George Benson	$14.95
00699072	Guitar Book of Pierre Bensusan	$29.95
00672331	Ron Carter – Acoustic Bass	$16.95
00672307	Stanley Clarke Collection	$19.95
00660115	Al Di Meola – Friday Night in San Francisco	$14.95
00604043	Al Di Meola – Music, Words, Pictures	$14.95
00673245	Jazz Style of Tal Farlow	$19.95
00672359	Bela Fleck and the Flecktones	$18.95
00699389	Jim Hall – Jazz Guitar Environments	$19.95
00699306	Jim Hall – Exploring Jazz Guitar	$19.95
00604049	Allan Holdsworth – Reaching for the Uncommon Chord	$14.95
00699215	Leo Kottke – Eight Songs	$14.95
00675536	Wes Montgomery – Guitar Transcriptions	$17.95
00672353	Joe Pass Collection	$18.95
00673216	John Patitucci	$16.95
00027083	Django Reinhardt Antholog	$14.95
00026711	Genius of Django Reinhardt	$10.95
00672374	Johnny Smith Guitar Solos	$16.95
00672320	Mark Whitfield	$19.95

PIANO & KEYBOARD

00672338	Monty Alexander Collection	$19.95
00672487	Monty Alexander Plays Standards	$19.95
00672318	Kenny Barron Collection	$22.95
00672520	Count Basie Collection	$19.95
00672364	Warren Bernhardt Collection	$19.95
00672439	Cyrus Chestnut Collection	$19.95
00673242	Billy Childs Collection	$19.95
00672300	Chick Corea – Paint the World	$12.95
00672537	Bill Evans at Town Hall	$16.95
00672425	Bill Evans – Piano Interpretations	$19.95
00672365	Bill Evans – Piano Standards	$19.95
00672510	Bill Evans Trio – Vol. 1: 1959-1961	$24.95
00672511	Bill Evans Trio – Vol. 2: 1962-1965	$24.95
00672512	Bill Evans Trio – Vol. 3: 1968-1974	$24.95
00672513	Bill Evans Trio – Vol. 4: 1979-1980	$24.95
00672381	Tommy Flanagan Collection	$24.99
00672492	Benny Goodman Collection	$16.95
00672486	Vince Guaraldi Collection	$19.95
00672419	Herbie Hancock Collection	$19.95
00672438	Hampton Hawes	$19.95

00672322	Ahmad Jamal Collection	$22.95
00672564	Best of Jeff Lorber	$17.99
00672476	Brad Mehldau Collection	$19.99
00672388	Best of Thelonious Monk	$19.95
00672389	Thelonious Monk Collection	$19.95
00672390	Thelonious Monk Plays Jazz Standards – Volume 1	$19.95
00672391	Thelonious Monk Plays Jazz Standards – Volume 2	$19.95
00672433	Jelly Roll Morton – The Piano Rolls	$12.95
00672553	Charlie Parker for Piano	$19.95
00672542	Oscar Peterson – Jazz Piano Solos	$16.95
00672544	Oscar Peterson – Originals	$9.95
00672532	Oscar Peterson – Plays Broadway	$19.95
00672531	Oscar Peterson – Plays Duke Ellington	$19.95
00672563	Oscar Peterson – A Royal Wedding Suite	$19.99
00672533	Oscar Peterson – Trios	$24.95
00672543	Oscar Peterson Trio – Canadiana Suite	$9.95
00672534	Very Best of Oscar Peterson	$22.95
00672371	Bud Powell Classics	$19.95
00672376	Bud Powell Collection	$19.95
00672437	André Previn Collection	$19.95
00672507	Gonzalo Rubalcaba Collection	$19.95
00672303	Horace Silver Collection	$19.95
00672316	Art Tatum Collection	$22.95
00672355	Art Tatum Solo Book	$19.95
00672357	Billy Taylor Collection	$24.95
00673215	McCoy Tyner	$16.95
00672321	Cedar Walton Collection	$19.95
00672519	Kenny Werner Collection	$19.95
00672434	Teddy Wilson Collection	$19.95

SAXOPHONE

00672566	The Mindi Abair Collection	$14.99
00673244	Julian "Cannonball" Adderley Collection	$19.95
00673237	Michael Brecker	$19.95
00672429	Michael Brecker Collection	$19.95
00672315	Benny Carter Plays Standards	$22.95
00672314	Benny Carter Collection	$22.95
00672394	James Carter Collection	$19.95
00672349	John Coltrane Plays Giant Steps	$19.95
00672529	John Coltrane – Giant Steps	$14.95
00672494	John Coltrane – A Love Supreme	$14.95
00672493	John Coltrane Plays "Coltrane Changes"	$19.95
00672453	John Coltrane Plays Standards	$19.95
00673233	John Coltrane Solos	$22.95
00672328	Paul Desmond Collection	$19.95
00672379	Eric Dolphy Collection	$19.95
00672530	Kenny Garrett Collection	$19.95
00699375	Stan Getz	$19.95
00672377	Stan Getz – Bossa Novas	$19.95
00672375	Stan Getz – Standards	$18.95
00673254	Great Tenor Sax Solos	$18.95

00672523	Coleman Hawkins Collection	$19.95
00673252	Joe Henderson – Selections from "Lush Life" & "So Near So Far"	$19.95
00672330	Best of Joe Henderson	$22.95
00673239	Best of Kenny G	$19.95
00673229	Kenny G – Breathless	$19.95
00672462	Kenny G – Classics in the Key of G	$19.95
00672485	Kenny G – Faith: A Holiday Album	$14.95
00672373	Kenny G – The Moment	$19.95
00672326	Joe Lovano Collection	$19.95
00672498	Jackie McLean Collection	$19.95
00672372	James Moody Collection – Sax and Flute	$19.95
00672416	Frank Morgan Collection	$19.95
00672539	Gerry Mulligan Collection	$19.95
00672352	Charlie Parker Collection	$19.95
00672561	Best of Sonny Rollins	$19.95
00672444	Sonny Rollins Collection	$19.95
00675000	David Sanborn Collection	$17.95
00672528	Bud Shank Collection	$19.95
00672491	New Best of Wayne Shorter	$19.95
00672550	The Sonny Stitt Collection	$19.95
00672350	Tenor Saxophone Standards	$18.95
00672567	The Best of Kim Waters	$17.99
00672524	Lester Young Collection	$19.95

TROMBONE

00672332	J.J. Johnson Collection	$19.95
00672489	Steve Turré Collection	$19.95

TRUMPET

00672557	Herb Alpert Collection	$14.99
00672480	Louis Armstrong Collection	$17.95
00672481	Louis Armstrong Plays Standards	$17.95
00672435	Chet Baker Collection	$19.95
00672556	Best of Chris Botti	$19.95
00672448	Miles Davis – Originals, Vol. 1	$19.95
00672451	Miles Davis – Originals, Vol. 2	$19.95
00672450	Miles Davis – Standards, Vol. 1	$19.95
00672449	Miles Davis – Standards, Vol. 2	$19.95
00672479	Dizzy Gillespie Collection	$19.95
00673214	Freddie Hubbard	$14.95
00672382	Tom Harrell – Jazz Trumpet	$19.95
00672363	Jazz Trumpet Solos	$9.95
00672506	Chuck Mangione Collection	$19.95
00672525	Arturo Sandoval – Trumpet Evolution	$19.95

FOR MORE INFORMATION, SEE YOUR LOCAL MUSIC DEALER, OR WRITE TO:

HAL•LEONARD®
CORPORATION
7777 W. BLUEMOUND RD. P.O. BOX 13819 MILWAUKEE, WI 53213

Visit our web site for a complete listing of our titles with songlists at
www.halleonard.com

0310